Level 1 Reiki for Kids

Tracie Talbott, Reiki Master Practitioner

Crystal Reiki Wellness

Crystal Reiki Wellness
901 Victory Lane
Excelsior Springs, Missouri 64024

www.crystalreikiwellness.com

Level 1 Reiki for Kids
Copyright © 2023 by Tracie Talbott
All rights reserved including the right of
reproduction in whole or in part in any form.
For educational and personal use only.

Illustrations created on Canva
www.canva.com

This book is dedicated to my children.
James and Leanna
Thank you for being my first Reiki students
and for inspiring me to create Reiki
educational material for kids.

"Reiki is a gift that can help children navigate their world with more ease and grace."
~ Pamela Miles ~

Contents

Dear Reiki Teachers,

I am glad that you have decided to teach Reiki to a child. I believe children are especially good at learning Reiki because they are so open-minded and often have more faith in the unseen than adults do. I think that we were all born with healing abilities that society taught us could not be real and so we lost them. Reiki has given us a system to work with to re-learn how to heal ourselves naturally. Children have not had time to get so far off track as some older people have, making it easier to them to get back on it.

Reiki can be a very valuable skill for children. It can empower them to deal with their own dis-ease, whether physical or emotional. It can work as a coping skill when they find themselves in tough situations and there isn't an adult available to help right away. Reiki can give them a sense of control in a world where they may feel they don't have a lot control over their lives.

I encourage you to read this book with your student, adding your personal thoughts, feelings, and experiences to the lessons along the way. If you are a Reiki Master, you can attune them when you feel they are ready. If you are not a Master Practitioner, you can still teach your student using this book. When you are finished, you can schedule a distance attunement for your student at https://crystalreikiwellness.as.me/kidsattunement.

This manual has been adapted from my signature product, the *Level 1 Reiki Kids Bundle*, a digital download on www.crystalreikiwellness.com. You can find additional Reiki Kids activities available for purchase on the website, in the *Reiki Kids Activity Bundle,* to expand on the lessons you will find in this book and provide your student with additional practice.

With Love and Light,

Tracie Eaves, Reiki Master Practitioner

Tips For Teaching Kids Reiki

1. **Keep it simple.** Everything we learned while training to become a Reiki practitioner, we can teach to our kids in simplified terms. Giving them the information in the form of short stories works well. Ask a lot of questions as you go to clarify that they understand the information you are giving them. When training my own children, I was talking to my daughter about getting grounded before doing spiritual work. She looked at me strangely, so I asked her if she remembered what getting grounded meant. She told me she did but wanted to know why I wanted her to get herself in trouble and not be able to leave the house before she does Reiki.

2. **Keep it short.** There is a lot of information to absorb about Reiki. Most of us who learned Reiki in the western part of the world, learned fairly quickly. Often, we are trained in as little as one weekend. It is not realistic to expect to keep younger children focused on learning Reiki for long stretches at time. When working with kids, I don't stress out about formality. I take my lead from them and watch their mood and attitude, so I know when best to take breaks, when to go into more detail, or to further simplify. My children and I went over one main concept a day and incorporated the information into our daily routine.

3. **Keep it fun.** Learning is always easier when you make it fun. Try to think of fun activities or experiments for children to do that go along with whatever lesson you are teaching them. For example, after teaching them about the energy, you can have them experiment with making energy/Ki balls. You could try giving them a gratitude exercise after teaching them the principle to be grateful. They can practice the hand positions on dolls or pets after learning about them. There are a lot of possibilities, just use your imagination.

Remember, the absolute best way to teach kids is through example. Let them see you practicing the Reiki hand positions and living by the Reiki Principles. Include them in your own daily Reiki routine. Show them how important it is to you and how it benefits your life, and they will likely want to experience it, too.

REIKI

What is Reiki?

Answering Questions About Reiki

What is Reiki?

Reiki is a way of using the energy in the world around us to keep ourselves and others healthy.

A man named Mikao Usui developed the kind of Reiki that we are learning about today, that is why it is called Usui Reiki. Some people have developed new kinds of Reiki based off of the ideas taught in Usui Reiki.

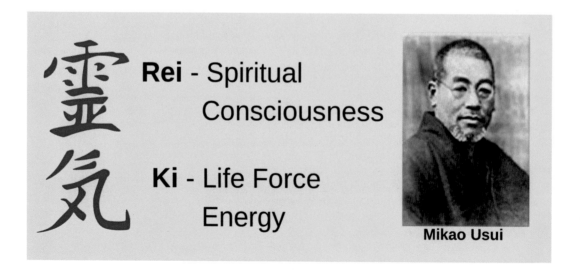

Rei - Spiritual Consciousness

Ki - Life Force Energy

Mikao Usui

What does Reiki do?

Our bodies already know how to heal themselves, but it is hard for them when we feel tense, afraid, angry, or bad about ourselves. Reiki helps by balancing our energy and allowing us to relax and feel good enough for our bodies to do the work of healing on their own.

How can Reiki be helpful?

Reiki helps us to...

- balance our energy.
- relax and calm down.
- feel happy and peaceful.
- heal faster when we are sick or hurt.
- feel more connected to our inner self and the world around us.
- be kinder to ourselves and others.
- focus and learn easier.

Can kids learn to do Reiki?

Yes! Anyone can learn to do Reiki no matter how young or old they are. It is never too early or too late to learn new ways to practice self-care or to care for others. It is important to take care of ourselves and the people we love, and learning Reiki is a great way to do that.

Is Reiki Magic?

No. Reiki is just a way of using the natural energy that all life is made out of. This energy surrounds us, is in us, and *is* us. Learning to use it to heal and promote wellness *can* seem like magic sometimes, though.

How do you learn to do Reiki?

A Reiki Master teaches you about Reiki. A Reiki Master might have given you this book. Reiki Masters teach their students how to use Reiki to help themselves and other people. When their students are ready, the Reiki Masters do a special ritual called an attunement that allows the student to tune into Reiki to use it for healing.

How does Reiki Work?

Reiki works by using our hands to channel energy that helps our body feel better. Think of it like drinking water through a straw - the water flows through the straw and into our body, just like the Reiki energy flows through our hands and into our body. The energy helps our body feel balanced and can even help it heal faster.

Now you know...

- What Reiki is.
- What Reiki does.
- How Reiki can help.
- How to learn Reiki.
- How Reiki works.

Reiki is a way to help your body and mind feel better. When you learn Reiki, you'll be able to use it anytime you need it, just like taking a sip from a straw whenever you're thirsty. Stay curious, keep learning, and always be kind to yourself and others. Continue reading to learn about the history of Reiki.

Usui Reiki History

Explaining Reiki History

Reiki History

About 100 years ago, there was a man named Mikao Usui. He was a Buddhist Monk and a very good and spiritual man. He liked learning about many things. He also liked helping people and worked at jobs where he could serve others.

Mikao Usui

Even though he was a good man, Mikao Usui was having a hard time. He was having some trouble with money and things weren't going very well for him. He wanted a better life for himself and he wanted to be able to better help other people, too. He decided he would go into the mountains of Mount Kurama for 21 days of training.

Mt. Kurama

No one knows for sure all that Mikao Usui did during his training. He probably spent a lot of time meditating. Meditating is a way to relax and clear your mind. It is a good way to feel connected to the world. Sometimes meditating will help people come up with answers to their problems.

Buddhist Mountain Meditation

During his training, Mikao Usui learned what he needed to know to start his Reiki practice. He became a Reiki Master. He was able to heal people with his hands and with special symbols. He spent some time helping and healing poor people. Then, he opened a clinic where he could heal people with Reiki and teach it to others so they could be healers, too.

Example of a Japanese Temple

Master Usui was not the only one to make Reiki what it is today. There were other great Reiki Masters. Master Hayashi helped make Reiki simpler for everyone to learn and use. Master Takata brought Reiki out of Japan and into our part of the world. The Reiki Masters that Master Takata trained spread Reiki out all over the world. Because of her it is practiced by many different people and in many different places and that's why you are able to learn about it today.

Master Hayashi

Master Takata

This story told of the history of Usui Reiki based on the research of Reiki Master, William Lee Rand. Now you know where Usui Reiki came from, and how it came to the West, so we can learn about it today.

Today, Reiki is used all over the world to help people feel better and stay healthy. And now that you know a little bit about the history of Reiki, you are ready to continue. Next you will learn about the energy body.

The Energy Body

The Chakras and Aura Explained

The Energy Body

Everything in the world is made of energy, including us. We have a physical body that we can see and we have an energy body that is invisible to us. Even though we can't see it, it is still important. When our energy body is healthy, it is easier to keep our physical body healthy.

The Energy Body

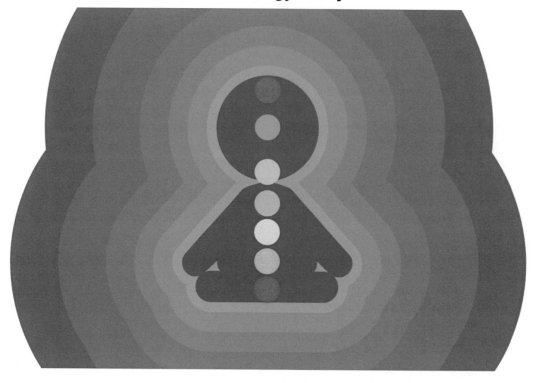

Chakras

Chakras are the energy centers of our bodies. There are seven major Chakras. They turn like wheels helping energy to run through us. When the Chakras are clear and balanced, the energy runs good and we stay healthy. When they get dirty or blocked, the energy doesn't run through them as well, and we can get sick.

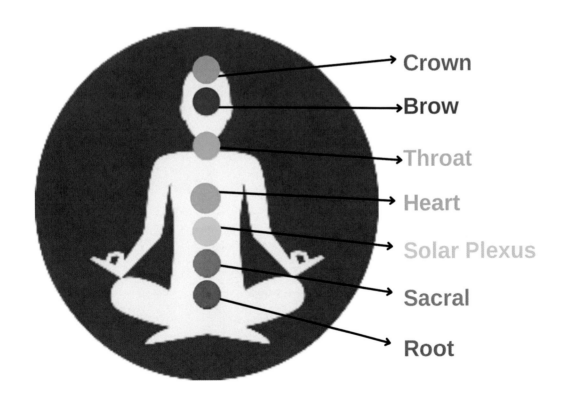

Crown

Brow

Throat

Heart

Solar Plexus

Sacral

Root

Root Chakra

The first Chakra is down by your bottom. It is called the Root Chakra. It keeps you rooted! When it is clear you feel safe and secure. When it gets blocked you might feel scared, worried, or feel like you don't fit in.

Red is good for this Chakra, so wearing red clothes, carrying red rocks, or eating red foods can help keep it clear. Spending time outside and playing sports are also good for the Root Chakra.

Sacral Chakra

The second Chakra is the Sacral Chakra. It is below your belly button. It has to do with your feelings. When it is clear you have better relationships and it is easier to be creative. When it gets blocked you might have trouble getting along with people and using your imagination could be harder.

The color orange is good for this Chakra. You can keep it clear with orange things. You can also help keep the Sacral Chakra healthy by dancing.

Solar Plexus Chakra

The third Chakra is the Solar Plexus Chakra. It is just a bit above your belly button. It has to do with your power. When it is clear, you will feel proud of who you are and it will be easier to do good things for yourself and others. When it is blocked, you might feel out of control and not make very good choices.

Yellow is a good color for this Chakra. Spending time in the sun can help keep it clear. Jogging is also a good way to keep the Solar Plexus Chakra healthy.

Heart Chakra

The fourth Chakra is the Heart Chakra. It is near your heart. This Chakra holds the love you have for yourself and the world. When it is clear you feel a lot of love for yourself and it is easy to be kind and loving to yourself and to others. When it is blocked it can make you feel lonely and sometimes can cause you to be too hard on yourself.

Green and pink are good colors for this Chakra. Listening to lovely music is a good way to keep it clear. Hugging and cuddling is also very good for the Heart Chakra.

Throat Chakra

The fifth Chakra is the Throat Chakra and it is near your throat. It has to do with communication. When it is clear it is easier to be true to yourself and to be honest with others. When it is blocked you might feel like pretending to be someone you are not or you may lie to yourself and others. It can make your throat hurt!

Blue is a good color for this Chakra. To keep it clear try to always be honest and say how you feel. Singing is a good way to help keep the Throat Chakra healthy.

Brow Chakra

The sixth Chakra is the Brow Chakra. Sometimes it is called the Third Eye Chakra. It is just above your eyes, in the center of your forehead. It has to do with your wisdom. When it is clear you are able to think clearly and sense things better. School work will feel easier. When it is blocked you might feel confused or get headaches.

Indigo, a purplish blue color, is good for this Chakra. Working on puzzles and reading are good for keeping this Chakra clear. It's also good for the Brow Chakra to never stop learning!

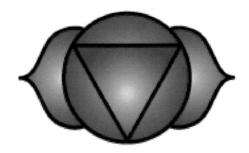

Crown Chakra

The seventh Chakra is the Crown Chakra. It has to do with your connection to Spirit or God. When it is clear you feel joy and happiness. It is easier to feel your connection to all of the things, plants, animals, and people in the world. When it is blocked you might feel really sad and alone.

Purple is a good color for this Chakra. Sitting still in the silence can help keep it clear. Getting a lot of rest is a good way to keep the Crown Chakra healthy.

31

Aura

The Aura is another part of the energy body. It is the energy that surrounds your body. When it is healthy, it can spread out very far from your body, but when it is not healthy it will be small and close to your body.

Some people can see the aura. A lot of people can feel it. Have you ever got a strange feeling when you are close to someone? That may have been because you were feeling their aura.

Grounding

When our energy body is not balanced with our physical body, we might start to feel strange. We might feel nervous or scared. We might get a tingling or buzzing feeling in our body.

Grounding is a way to balance our energy body with our physical body. When we are grounded, we feel connected to our physical body and to the world we live in. We can get grounded by focusing on our breath, spending time in nature, and by paying attention to what is around us.

Now you know...

- What the seven major Chakras are.
- About the Aura.
- What grounding is.

    I hope you enjoyed learning about the energy body and how it can affect our health. Learning about the energy body helps us to better understand our health and makes it easier for us to take care of ourselves. Now you are ready to learn about the Reiki Principles.

Just for today...

The Reiki Principles

A guide for getting and staying healthy.

Reiki Principles

The reiki Principles were Master Usui's guide for getting and staying healthy. He believed that if we say these words every morning and every night it would help us to live in a way that would keep us happy and healthy. He taught that we should speak them out loud and feel them in our hearts.

The Reiki Principles

Just for today, do not anger.
Just for today, don't worry about things.
Just for today, be thankful.
Just for today, be honest and work hard.
Just for today, be kind to everyone.

Just for today...

"Just for today" is a special phrase that is part of the Reiki Principles. It reminds us to focus on being kind, respectful, and compassionate to ourselves and others, just for today. We don't need to worry about the future or the past, we just need to try to be our best selves today. By doing this, we can make each day a little better for ourselves and those around us.

Just for today!

Just for today, do not anger.

Everyone gets angry sometimes. That's okay. Anger lets us know that we are not okay with something. After we get the message that something isn't okay, we can let go of the anger and work on fixing the problem.

If we hold on to angry feelings they can start to make us feel sick. Angry feelings can also make it hard to get along with other people.

Just for today, don't worry.

It can be hard not to worry about things. We might worry about making mistakes or worry that something bad will happen. Worrying doesn't stop those things from happening, though. Sometimes worrying too much can even cause us to start making mistakes!

We need to trust that things will always work out exactly the way they are supposed to for us to learn everything that we need to know. We can learn a lot from things that seem bad. Just remember, bad times won't last forever. Things get better. Be hopeful.

Just for today, I will be thankful.

There are so many things to be thankful for! When we are thankful for the good things in our life, life will give us more good things. It is really amazing how much good we can attract with gratitude!

Spend time thinking about the things you are thankful for. Give thanks to the world for all the good things that are in it. Remember to say thank you to the people who do nice things for you, care for you, and make sure you have the things you need.

Just for today, I will be honest and work hard.

    Being honest makes life a lot easier. When we are honest, people can get to know us better and feel like they can trust us. We also make ourselves and the people who care about us proud when we work hard to be our best and make good choices.

When we are not honest we might feel bad about it. Those bad feelings can cause us to get sick. Each day we should work hard to learn, grow, and be the best we can be.

Just for today, I will be kind.

Kindness is very important. When we are kind we make the world a better place. When we are kind we make people feel good and we can feel good about ourselves. If we make other people feel good, it is easier for them to be kind, too. This is how kindness spreads.

We need to be kind to ourselves and others. Kindness can fill our hearts with love. Nothing can keep us healthy and happy better than love!

Now you know...

- What the Reiki Principles are.
- Why the Reiki Principles are important.
- How living by the Reiki Principles can make life better.

Try to say the Reiki Principles out loud every morning when you get up and every night before you go to bed. You can also say them if you start to feel angry or worried or you are having a hard time being thankful, honest, or kind. Saying them can make it easier to calm down and make good choices. When we make good choices it helps to keep us happy and healthy.

Healing Hands

Healing with Reiki

A guide for healing the Self and Others with Reiki

How Reiki Heals

After a Reiki Master attunes a student to Level 1 Reiki, they can use their hands to channel Reiki. We can give Reiki to ourselves and to others by putting our hands gently on or right above certain places on the body. We always wear clothes when doing Reiki and never touch private parts. Reiki can help us feel better when we are tired, sick, hurt, frustrated, or scared.

Getting Ready

After you are attuned to Level 1 Reiki by a Reiki Master, you can use your hands to help yourself and others heal with Reiki. There are some things you will need to do to get ready to do Reiki.

1. Wash your hands.
2. Get grounded.
3. Put your hands together in front of your chest.
4. Say "thank you" for Reiki.
5. Think about opening up to Reiki.Try saying, "I'm ready to channel Reiki now." Or, you can say anything that feels right to you.

Hand Placements for Self-Healing

When you are ready, you will put your hands in certain places for the energy to flow. The energy will go where it is needed most. To do self-healing you will put your hands on different spots on your own body. These are called hand placements. You will put your hands in each position for a few minutes or for however long feels right. Some Reiki Masters may teach these positions a little differently and that is okay.

Self-Healing
Reiki Hand Placements

1

2

3

4

5

6

7

8

9

10

11

12

Hand Placements for Healing Others

The hand placements are also used to heal others by placing your hands on or just above their body. Remember, each Reiki Master may teach the hand positions in a slightly different way.

Always ask permission before giving anyone Reiki or touching them. Never, ever touch anyone in their private areas or anywhere that makes them uncomfortable. Explain to them what you will do and where you will touch them. Tell them to drink lots of water and rest afterward.

Reiki Hand Placements
for Treating Others

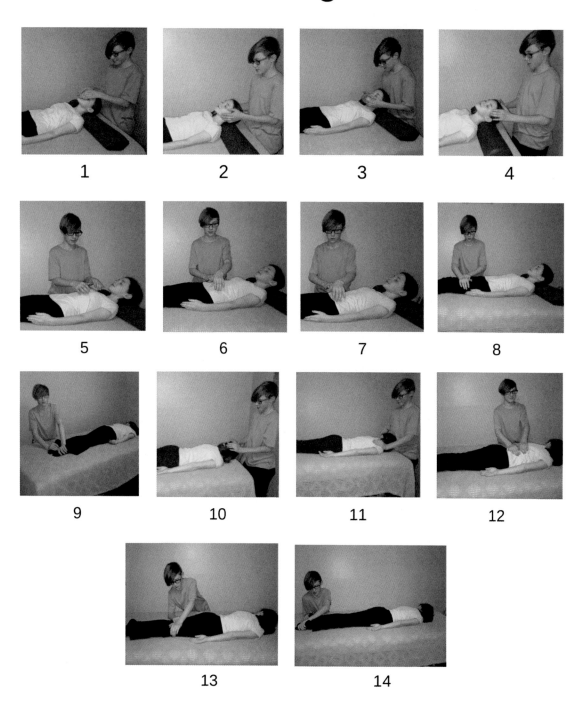

Cleaning the Aura

After you do the hand placements, you can clean the Aura. To do this, just run your hands down the body like you are trying to brush off some dust or snow. When you are done, touch your hands to the floor. This wipes away any extra energy and gives it back to the Earth.

Things to Remember

Remember, you get better and stronger at everything when you practice. If you practice Reiki everyday it will help keep you happy and healthy.

Here are some tips…

- Always drink lots of water.
- Relax and enjoy life.
- Eat healthy foods and get lots of exercise.
- Even when you use Reiki, you still need to visit doctors and take their advice, too.
- Keep learning!

Now you know...

- How to get ready to do Reiki.
- All about Reiki hand placements.
- About self-healing.
- About healing others.
- About cleaning the Aura.

You have now learned all about getting ready to do Reiki and you know how to use your hands to help yourself and others feel better. Now you are ready to learn about attunements.

What is an Attunement?

Answering Questions About Attunements.

What is a Reiki Attunement?

An attunement is how a Reiki Master passes Reiki on to their student. They tune their student into Reiki like tuning the television to a certain channel to watch the show you want.

After the student has been given an attunement by a Reiki Master they will be able to practice Reiki, too. There are three levels of Reiki attunements.

What are the different levels of Reiki?

Level 1 Reiki teaches us to begin to connect with Reiki and use it to heal ourselves and people we love.

Level 2 Reiki teaches special symbols and how to use Reiki in different ways and send it to different times and places. We should practice Level 1 Reiki for a while before learning Level 2.

Level 3 Reiki teaches us how to pass Reiki on to others and how to teach it to them. You should practice for a long time before learning Level 3 Reiki.

How do you get ready for an attunement?

A few days before an attunement you should spend a lot of time playing outside and not watch much TV or play video games. Spend some time just being quiet and resting.

You should take good care of yourself before an attunement by eating good, healthy food and not too much sugar or fat. You should also drink a lot of water.

What happens after an attunement?

You should drink lots of water and rest as much as you need to after an attunement. You might feel a little funny while you get used to Reiki and start to heal. Let your parents or Reiki Teacher know how you are feeling.

It is important to do self-Reiki for 3 weeks after an attunement. You will need to practice the self-healing hand placements every day for 21 days.

Now you know...

- What an attunement is.
- The levels of Reiki
- How to get ready for an attunement.
- What to do after an attunement.

Congratulations! You have learned all about Reiki attunements. Now you are almost ready to start your journey as a Reiki practitioner. Remember, practicing Reiki means you are helping yourself and others feel better. Keep an open heart and mind, and always trust your intuition. You are on your way to becoming a confident and compassionate healer.

Reiki Activities

Activities to practice what's been learned.

Activities

     To finish up our time together, I want to share ten activities with you to help you practice the things you have learned. The following activities will give you a chance to play with energy, practice Reiki, and take good care of yourself.

21 Days of Self-Reiki

After your attunement, you should do self-Reiki every day for 21 days. This helps you get used to Reiki and helps you begin healing. Color in one circle after you've finished giving yourself Reiki each day.

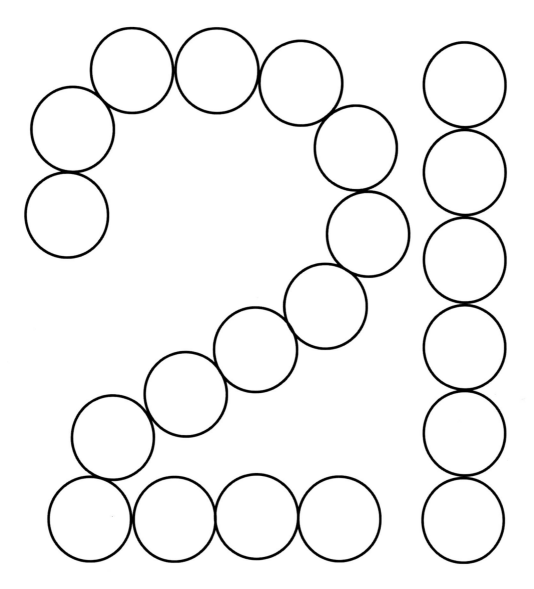

Create an Energy Ball

This is a fun exercise to experiment with life energy.

You can create a ball of energy with your hands. The more you practice, the easier it gets. It can be fun to play with the energy to get to know how it feels.

1. Stand up straight and relax.
2. Take a few deep breaths.
3. Rub your hands together fast until they feel warm.
4. Hold your hands in front of you, about one inch apart.
5. Slowly move your hands just far enough apart to hold a small ball.
6. Move your hands slowly in and out until it feels like the air between them gets thicker. The thick feeling is the energy gathering.
7. Form the energy into a ball the way you pack a snowball.

Pet Reiki

A guide for giving pets Reiki.

Our pets like Reiki too! You can offer your pet Reiki anytime you want. If they stay close, keep giving it to them. If they try to move away, offer again later.

1. Sit or stand near your pet.
2. Tell your pet you are going to offer it Reiki.
3. Get grounded.
4. Give thanks.
5. Open yourself to Reiki.
6. Gently and slowly stroke your pet with your hands while sending Reiki or put your hands on your pet's cage or tank.
7. Give your pet Reiki for as long as they seems to want it.
8. Thank your pet for letting you share Reiki with it and thank Reiki for helping your pet.

Reiki Rice

The Reiki Rice Experiment is a fun and easy way to experiment with Reiki after you are attuned.

What you will need:

1. Two clear, empty jars or bottles with lids
2. Two cups of uncooked white rice
3. One and a half cups of water
4. A permanent marker

Use the permanent marker to label 1 container "Reiki." Label the other container "control". Fill each container with 1 cup of uncooked rice and 3/4 cup of water. For 2 weeks, give Reiki to the "Reiki" container of rice for at least 10 minutes a day. Do not give Reiki to the "control" container. At the end of the week compare the Rice. Does the Reiki Rice look better than the regular rice? Try this when you first start Reiki and again when you are more experienced. See if there is a difference.

Reiki Rocks

   Reiki Rocks are a fun and inexpensive way for Reiki Kids to show kindness. You can use rocks that you find outside or you can use crystals or gemstones to make Reiki Rocks.

1. Gather some rocks that fit nicely in your hand and feel good to hold.
2. Place the rocks in bowl.
3. Get grounded.
4. Give thanks.
5. Open yourself to Reiki.
6. Put your hands gently on each side of the bowl.
7. Give the bowl of rocks Reiki for about 15 minutes while thinking kind thoughts.
8. Give the Reiki Rocks to people you know or leave them in different places for strangers to find.

Your Busy Mind

Just for today, do not get angry and do not worry.

The Reiki Principles tell us not to get angry or worry. That can be really hard! Anger and worry are natural emotions and it is okay to feel them. After we feel them, we need to calm ourselves down though, so we can think clearly and make good choices. This project can help us to calm ourselves down.

What you will need:

1. A clear, empty jar or bottle with lid
2. Half of a 5 oz bottle of clear glue
3. 2 tablespoons Glitter
4. Warm water
5. A grown up with hot glue to seal the lid

Put the glue into the bottle or jar. Add the glitter. Then, fill the bottle or jar the rest of the way up with warm water. Have a grown up use hot glue to seal the lid back onto the bottle or jar.

69

After you've finished putting everything together, shake the jar up. Shake it really good! Watch the way the glitter swirls around and around inside the container. Your thoughts and feelings swirl around in your mind in the same way. It's hard to see clearly through the glitter isn't it? It can be hard to see things clearly and make good choices with too many thoughts and feeling swirling in our mind.

Now hold the container still and watch as the glitter starts to slow down and settle to the bottom. When we focus on the glitter, our thoughts and feelings slow down, too. This helps us to stay calm and think clearly.

5-4-3-2-1 .... Get Grounded!

One way to take care of your energy body is by grounding. When you get grounded you are in touch with your body and the space around you. Use this activity to get grounded by focusing on your senses.

Take a moment to find...

5 things you can *see*.

4 things you can *feel*.

3 things you can *hear*.

2 things you can *smell*.

1 thing you can *taste*.

Lazy 8 Breathing

Just for today, do not anger or worry.

When you feel angry or worried you can trying using this breathing exercise to calm down. When we focus on our breath it causes our mind and body to relax.

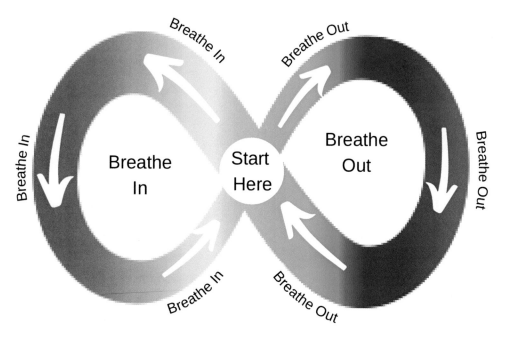

- Go up to the left and trace the left part of the 8 with your finger while you breathe in.
- When you get to the middle of the 8 again, breathe out while you trace the right part of the 8.
- Continue breathing around the Lazy 8 until you have a calm body and mind.

Stay Connected with Reiki Rope

When you can't be with the people you love, do you ever feel sad or disconnected from them? When you are missing someone, Reiki can help! Use this Reiki exercise to help you feel connected with the people you love, even when they are far away.

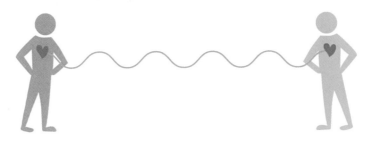

1. Think about the person you are missing and picture them in your mind.
2. Imagine a magical rope that connects your heart to theirs. See the rope connecting you in your mind. What color is it? Does it glow or glitter?
3. Put your hands over your heart and send Reiki into your own heart and then through the rope to the person you love for a few minutes.
4. Remember that the rope is still connecting you to your loved one even after you have stopped sending Reiki. You are always connected and never really apart.

Make Friends with a Tree

Trees help to keep our air clean and filter water in the ground. They make a home for birds, insects, animals, and other types of plant life. Trees can also help us feel more connected to nature.

Go for a walk and pay attention to the trees around you. Find one you like and make friends with it. Below are some ideas. Go back and vist your new tree friend often.

1. Talk to the tree. Trees are great listeners and never tell your secrets. You can tell it anything you want.

2. Use your heart to listen to the tree. What do you think it would tell you if it could talk?

3. Put your hands on the tree and offer it Reiki.

4. Put your hands on the tree and ask it to help you ground and connect with the Earth.

Dear Reiki Students,

Congratulations! You have completed Level 1 Reiki for Kids. Did you enjoy learning about Reiki and practicing the activities in this book? Let me know by sending me email to Tracie@crystalreikiwellness.com to tell me about it or to ask me any questions you still have. I would love to hear from you!

I hope that you learned a lot about Reiki and that you decide to keep learning and to keep practicing.

With love and light,

Reiki Master Tracie

About the Author

Tracie Talbott is a Reiki Master Practitioner and Life Coach. She has been practicing Reiki and crystal healing since 2016. After teaching her own kids Reiki, she decided to publish the Level 1 Reiki Kids Bundle in 2019 so that other Reiki teachers would have everything they need to teach Reiki to kids. She believes that Reiki is a great self-care tool for everyone.

Tracie has 5 children of her own and 2 grandchildren. She lives near Kansas City, Missouri with her two youngest kids and her husband, Dan. They like to travel and enjoy the beauty of nature. Spiritual practice is an important part of their family life.

Master Tracie